SPORTS ZONE

SOCCER

A Guide for Players and Fans

BY HEATHER WILLIAMS

CAPSTONE PRESS
a capstone imprint

Fact Finders Books are published by Capstone
1710 Roe Crest Drive, North Mankato, Minnesota 56003
www.capstonepub.com

Editorial Credits
Lauren Dupuis-Perez, editor; Sara Radka, designer;
Eric Gohl, media researcher; Laura Manthe, production specialist

Photo Credits
Getty Images: Buda Mendes, cover (foreground), Catherine Ivill, 17,
Dan Mullan, 23, Dean Mouhtaropoulos, 28 (bottom), EyeEm / Zhihua
Hu, 11 (front), fstop123, 29, Ian Walton, 19, Jamie Squire, 25, Jasper
Juinen, 22, Laurence Griffiths, 24, Matthias Hangst, 4, Michael Reaves,
20, SerrNovik, 28 (top), monkeybusinessimages, cover (background),
Steve Debenport, 27, The Good Brigade, 14; Pixabay: intographics,
background; Shutterstock: Eugene Onischenko, 10-11, Goran Bogicevic,
12 (bottom), imstock, 12 (top), OSTILL is Franck Camhi, 18, Who is
Danny, 8-9; Wikimedia: State Library of South Australia, 7, Unknown, 9,
www.twylah.com, 6

Library of Congress Cataloging-in-Publication Data
Names: Williams, Heather author.
Title: Soccer : a guide for players and fans / by Heather Williams.
Description: First Edition. | North Mankato, Minnesota : An imprint of
Capstone Press, [2019] | Series: Fact Finders. Sports Zone
Identifiers: LCCN 2019005984 | ISBN 9781543574296 (Hardcover) |
ISBN 9781543574616 (Paperback) | ISBN 9781543574302 (eBook PDF)
Subjects: LCSH: Soccer—Juvenile literature. | Soccer for
children—Juvenile literature.
Classification: LCC GV943.25 .W54 2019 | DDC 796.334—dc23
LC record available at https://lccn.loc.gov/2019005984

All internet sites in the back matter were available and accurate when
this book was sent to press.

Printed in the United States   5739

TABLE OF CONTENTS

INTRODUCTION

Paul Pogba helped lead France to a 2018 World Cup victory. Pogba scored one of his team's goals during its 4–2 final win over Croatia.

Soccer teams from countries around the world compete in the World Cup every four years. The international soccer **tournament** attracts huge crowds of devoted fans. The World Cup is so popular that one country built a brand-new city for it! In Qatar, the city of Lusail did not even exist in 2005. Since then, it has grown from a tiny village to a huge city with skyscrapers and shopping malls. Qatar is building nine brand-new stadiums for the 2022 World Cup.

More people watch the World Cup on TV than the Super Bowl. American players like Christian Pulisic and Alex Morgan are exciting to watch. Superstars like Lionel Messi from Argentina and Neymar from Brazil keep soccer in the spotlight. In 2017, there were 800,000 high school soccer players in the United States. More than 2 million U.S. kids ages 6 to 12 play youth soccer. People of all ages love watching and playing soccer.

tournament—a contest in which the winner is the one who wins the most games

Harry Thickett played for Sheffield United in the late 1800s and early 1900s.

Soccer is called "football" in most countries outside the United States. People have been playing some form of soccer for many centuries. However, the sport as we now know it started in England in the 1800s. A group of players there decided football needed clearer rules. They did not like the way some people played. The game often got rough and sometimes included shin-kicking, tripping, and even biting. Also, some players often picked up the ball and ran with it. The group decided on rules and founded the Football Association (FA) in 1863. The FA was the first professional soccer league in the world.

league — a group of sports teams that play against each other

Teams started forming all over Great Britain. British sailors and traders taught the game to people in countries they visited. Soccer became popular across Europe. Also, people in Mexico and South America started playing. By 1904, there were many soccer teams around the world. The Fédération

Historians have called the 1920s the "Golden Age of Sports." Soccer gained popularity, and new teams were formed around the world.

Internationale de Football Association (FIFA) was founded to make sure all the teams follow the rules. FIFA also plans tournaments, such as the World Cup.

Soccer was one of the first sports to build large stadiums to host games. Many countries now have professional soccer leagues. Major League Soccer (MLS) is the home of professional soccer in the United States and Canada. MLS was founded in 1996. There are 24 MLS teams today. The National Women's Soccer League (NWSL) started in 2012. There are nine NWSL teams.

The United States has **national teams** for men and women. The U.S. Women's National Team is the most successful women's team of all time. They have won three World Cups, four Olympic gold medals, and many other minor international tournaments. At the 1999 FIFA Women's World Cup, about 90,000 people came to watch the them play China. It was a record high for women's sports.

Today, most middle and high schools and many colleges in the United States have soccer teams. There are community and club teams in cities across the country. There are even programs for kids as young as 18 months old.

FACT

In the original rules of soccer, written in 1863, there was no height requirement for the goal. A player could score a goal as long as the ball passed between two goal posts. This is similar to a field goal in American football.

national team — a team chosen to represent the country where the players live

1863

1904

1930

1991

2012

After hundreds of years of a rough and rowdy form of the game, the Football Association is established to bring order to soccer.

Fédération Internationale de Football Association is founded to oversee the growth of soccer around the world.

The first World Cup for men's soccer is played. The United States wins third place. This is the best the U.S. men's national team has ever done at the World Cup.

The U.S. Women's National Team wins the first ever women's World Cup. U.S. legend and team captain Michelle Akers scores both of the USWNT's goals to defeat Norway 2–1 in the final.

The National Women's Soccer League is formed 19 years after the men's MLS. The founding team, the Portland Thorns Football Club, has since won the NWSL championship two times.

The First World Cup

The first World Cup took place in 1930. It was held in Uruguay in South America. The team from Uruguay had won the gold medal at the 1928 Olympics. Uruguay was building soccer stadiums and had lots of room for the World Cup. Uruguay paid for 12 other teams to come to the tournament. Teams came from Europe, North America, and South America. Uruguay won the final game against Argentina.

ESSENTIAL EQUIPMENT

Not much equipment was needed to play the very first soccer games. Players only had two pieces of equipment, a goal and a ball. Early balls were made from animal skins. Some were pig bladders filled with air! The first rubber ball that could be filled with air was made in 1862. The FA made the first official soccer ball design. Today, players need a few more items to play in a soccer game. Special socks and shoes and some safety gear are required.

1. Ball

Every team needs a ball. Soccer balls come in size 3, 4, or 5 depending on age. Size 5 balls are used by the players' age 12 and older.

2. Socks

Soccer socks help protect lower legs and keep shin guards in place. All players on a team have to wear matching soccer socks except the goalkeeper.

3. Shin Guards

Hard plastic shields protect shins and ankles from kicks. No player is allowed to step on the field without them.

4. Cleats

Soccer cleats have rubber studs or spikes on the bottom. They help players run on grass without slipping.

5. Goal

Every game has a goal. The size depends on the age of the players, but standard goals are 8 feet high (2.4 meters) and 8 yards (7.3 m) wide. Goals are usually made of a metal frame and a cloth net.

5

Shin guards protect parts of the leg that are not protected by muscle or tissue.

Gear for the Game

A few safety items are required for soccer. Players can wear other gear if they choose. Shin guards are the number-one required safety gear for players. They are made of hard plastic. Shin guards fit over the lower legs. They keep players' shins and ankles safe from hard kicks. Players usually attach shin guards to their legs with soft straps. Special soccer socks hold them in place. Players of all ages and levels have to wear shin guards. All players must wear special shoes called cleats. Cleats have studs on the bottom. They help players run on grass.

FACT

The first rubber soccer ball was invented in 1855 by Charles Goodyear. It was brown. The popular black-and-white paneled ball did not hit fields until the 1960s.

Some soccer players choose to wear protective headgear. Padded helmets that look like wide headbands protect the skull. Soccer players can injure their brain when they use their heads to pass the ball. This is called heading. They can also bump heads with another player. This can cause a **concussion**. Headgear can keep concussions from happening. Some players also wear sports goggles and mouthguards. Sports goggles are padded glasses that keep the eyes safe. A mouthguard is a piece of rubber that fits over the teeth.

The goalkeeper on a team has extra gear. They wear special gloves to grip the ball. They can also wear padded pants and shirts. Goalies also wear different colored jerseys, shorts, and socks. This way the teams can tell the goalies apart from other players.

Tsu Chu (or Cuju)

One of the earliest forms of soccer was called *tsu' chu* or *cuju*. It was played in China more than 2,000 years ago. The game was part of the training program for Chinese soldiers. *Tsu* means "kicking with feet" and *chu* means "ball." Players had to kick a ball through a small hole in a net 30 feet (9 m) above the field. Even though the gear has not changed much, today's players are lucky the net is on the ground!

concussion — an injury to the brain caused by a hard blow to the head

In youth soccer team sizes range from no more than 4 players to no more than 11 players per team, depending on the age.

There were no rules in the very first soccer games. Today there are 17 basic rules of soccer. Some rules keep players safe. Others make sure players everywhere understand how the game works. There are also rules about how many players can be on the field.

A team has 10 field players and a goalkeeper. Youth teams can have as few as four field players. The goalie is the only player who can pick up the ball on the field. Goalies try to keep the ball from going into the goal. Teams also have defenders who play in front of the goal. Defenders try to keep the ball away from their own goal. Midfielders play between the defenders and forwards. They can help defend the goal. They can also score. Forwards are the players who score most of the goals. They play closest to the other team's goal.

A soccer field is called a pitch. Every pitch has sidelines, goal lines, and **penalty** areas painted on the ground. If a ball goes out on a sideline, a player throws it back into the game. This is called a throw-in. If a player kicks the ball out of bounds at his or her own goal line, the other team gets a corner kick. If a player kicks the ball across the other team's goal line, the other team gets a goal kick.

Most soccer games are 90 minutes long. The game is split into two 45-minute halves with a halftime break in between. Youth games usually have 20- to 35-minute halves. The length of time depends on the age group. In most games, a **tie** is okay. In tournaments, there is extra time added called overtime. If the game is still tied after overtime, a penalty kick shootout takes place. Players get to shoot the ball from a spot 12 yards (11 m) from the goal.

penalty—a punishment for breaking the rules
tie—when a game ends with both sides having the same score

If a player from one team kicks a ball out of bounds, a player from the other team is awarded a throw-in from the spot the ball left the field. A player throws the ball in from outside of the field boundaries to members of their team. A goal cannot be scored by throwing the ball into the net.

Players sometimes get to take penalty and free kicks during a game. This happens when a major rule is broken. Two of the most common reasons for penalties are handballs and fouls inside the goalie box.

If the ball touches any part of a player's arm it is called a handball. Players are also not allowed to kick, shove, trip, hold, or elbow another player. These are called fouls. If a handball or foul is called on the field, the other team gets a chance to kick the ball.

A professional soccer match might have 20 to 30 fouls.

From the sidelines, referee assistants hold a flag in different positions to signal throw-ins, substitutions, and offsides.

During a soccer game, a player is not allowed to kick the ball to a teammate who is closer to the goal than the other team's second-to-last defender. This is called being offsides. Before the offsides rule, players could stay in front of the other team's goal and wait for the ball to come to them. This made scoring too easy.

STRATEGIES TO SUCCEED

Midfielder Phil Foden (left) is known for being a mobile player, with strong dribbling skills. Foden was a part of Manchester City's youth program until joining the team in 2017 at the age of 17.

A soccer team has two jobs. One is to score goals. The other is to keep the other team from scoring. When a team is trying to score it is called offense. When a team is trying to stop the other team from scoring it is called defense.

Trapping and controlling the ball are important for both offense and defense. Trapping means that a player uses his or her body to stop the ball. Players can use any part of the body except the arms and hands to trap the ball. Once a player traps the ball, it is important to control it. Players can **dribble** or pass the ball. Players can dribble without looking at the ball. A player must be able to look around and find the best teammate to receive a pass. Kicking the ball to a teammate is called passing. Passes can be to nearby teammates or across the field.

dribble — to move the ball along by kicking it with your feet

A team that has control of the ball is the offensive team. They are moving the ball toward their opponents' goal. A team on offense never stops moving. Players pass and then keep moving so they can be a target for a pass. By moving into open spaces, players can create chances to score.

Sometimes defenders keep the offense from passing the ball. An offensive team can switch fields when this happens. Switching fields means making a long pass or several short passes to a teammate who is on the other side of the field. It can also be a pass backward toward the player's own goal. The goalie can then kick a long ball to the other side of the field. Switching fields lets the offense find a new path to the goal.

Forward Cristiano Ronaldo averages at least one goal per game.

A corner kick has similar rules to a throw-in, except it is awarded when a defending player kicks the ball out of bounds on the goal line. The team playing offense then is allowed to kick from a marked area at the corner of the field.

The offensive team can also use throw-ins and corner kicks to score. These are called set-pieces. Teams can set up plays for their offense during set-pieces. For example, four or five players can line up in front of the goal and be ready to score during their team's corner kick.

During the 2018 Football Association Challenge Cup Final match in 2018, Chelsea forward Eden Hazard broke through Manchester United's defense. A penalty kick by Hazard led to Chelsea's 1–0 win.

It is fun to score, but teams need a good defense to win a soccer game. Some soccer teams use man-to-man defense. This means each player guards a player from the other team. Usually a team's midfielders guard the other team's midfielders. Defenders guard the opponent's forwards, and forwards guard the opponent's defenders.

When defending, a player should always try and be closer to their own goal than the attacker. This is an important part of defense in soccer. It is called being goal side. Strong defenders stay close to the player they are defending. This forces the player to pass the ball. Stealing the ball from a player who is dribbling is called a tackle.

When a defender gets the ball, he or she can pass it to another defender or clear the ball out of the area. Most defenders choose to clear the ball or kick it toward their own midfielders or forwards. This gives the offense time to set up and take control of the ball.

Abby Wambach

Abby Wambach is one of the most famous soccer players of all time. Wambach played soccer at the University of Florida and scored 96 goals for the team, a record that has not been broken. Wambach was part of the U.S. Women's National Team for 14 years. She played forward and was known for scoring goals with her head. She holds the record for most goals scored for a country by any player, male or female. Wambach scored a total of 184 goals for the United States.

READY TO PLAY?

Kids who want to play soccer are in luck! Soccer is one of the most popular outdoor youth sports in the United States. Watching soccer is a great way to learn the rules and positions. Kids can watch MLS and NWSL games on TV. They can also watch a live game. There are games at local high schools and colleges in cities across the country.

Players new to the game need to practice the basics. Dribbling the ball with your feet and gaining more ball control through practice is important. Local parks with soccer fields are a great place to practice running with a soccer ball. Starting **pickup** games is another way to improve.

Running and exercising will help the body get stronger. Soccer players run a lot! Drinking lots of water helps the body work properly. Eating well is important too. Being in great shape will make playing on a soccer team much easier.

pickup — a type of game that is played just for fun

Soccer practice typically lasts about an hour. A coach might decide to spend 10 minutes warming up, 20 minutes working on technique and skills, and 30 minutes on team games or free play.

Joining a Team

New players can sign up with a club or community team. These teams have programs for boys and girls of all ages. School teams usually start in middle school. Many cities have summer and weekend camps so players can work on skills.

Getting the right equipment is important. A salesperson at a sporting goods store can make sure players get correct sizes. Every player needs his or her own ball, shin guards, and cleats. Most teams give players a jersey to wear in games. Players will need a few pairs of soccer socks and athletic shorts.

FACT

Nooit Opgeven Altijd Doorzetten, Aangenaam Door Vermaak En Nuttig Door Ontspanning, Combinatie Breda is the full name of a professional soccer team in the Netherlands. In English, the name means "Never give up, always persevere, pleasant for its entertainment and useful for its relaxation, Combination Breda." It is one of the longest team names in the world.

In 2018, about 2.3 million U.S. kids played youth soccer.

Kids just starting out should be willing to learn more than one position. Knowing how to play defensive and offensive positions helps players get better. The most important rule is to have fun. Learning a new sport can be hard. However, playing on a team is a great way to learn and make new friends.

Glossary

concussion *(kuhn-KUH-shuhn)*—an injury to the brain caused by a hard blow to the head

dribble *(DRI-buhl)*—to move the ball along by kicking it with your feet

league *(LEEG)*—a group of sports teams that play against each other

penalty *(PEN-uhl-tee)*—a punishment for breaking the rules

pickup *(PIK-up)*—a type of game that is played just for fun

national team *(NASH-uh-nuhl TEEM)*—a team chosen to represent the country where the players live

tie *(TYE)*—when a game ends with both sides having the same score

tournament *(TUR-nuh-muhnt)*—a contest in which the winner is the one who wins the most games

Read More

Hoena, B. A. *Everything Soccer.* Washington, D.C.: National Geographic Society, 2014.

Hornby, Hugh. *Soccer.* DK Eyewitness Books. New York: DK Publishing, 2018.

Terrell, Brandon. *Soccer Showdown: U.S.* Women's Stunning 1999 World Cup Win. Greatest Sports Moments. North Mankato, MN: Capstone Press, 2019.

Internet Sites

Soccer (Football)
www.ducksters.com/sports/soccer.php

Sports Illustrated Kids Soccer
www.sikids.com/soccer

FIFA
https://www.fifa.com/

Index